40 DAYS FAST
A 40 Day Devotional

Stephen Hoover

40 Days Fast: A 40 Day Devotional

Copyright © 2013 by Stephen Hoover

Library of Congress Control Number: 2013922650

Book design by: Cat Stewart

Cover design by: 2Faced Design

All rights reserved. No part of this book may be used or reproduced in any manner whatsoever including Internet usage, without written permission of the author.

ISBN: 9781941084076

Dedicated to my mother, Judy C. Hoover, with love.

Table of Contents

PART I: THE RACE 1

DAY 1: 1

1 CORINTHIANS 9:24-27 2

- FINDING YOUR GOAL 2
- TRAINING 2
- SPEAKING TO OTHERS WITHOUT DISQUALIFICATION 3
- FINAL THOUGHTS 3

DAY 2: 5

ECCLESIASTES 9:11-12 5

- LOOKING AT LIFE 6
- THE RACE IN THE WORLD 6
- FINAL THOUGHTS 8

DAY 3: 9

JOHN 16:33 9

- PERSONAL CHALLENGES 10
- COLLECTIVE CHALLENGES 11
- FINAL THOUGHTS 11

DAY 4: 13

2 TIMOTHY 1:7 13

- POWER OVER TIMIDITY 13
- LOVE 14
- SELF-DISCIPLINE 15
- FINAL THOUGHTS 15

DAY 5: 17

PSALM 119:71 17

- LEARNING FROM INDIVIDUAL TROUBLES 18
- LEARNING FROM TROUBLES COLLECTIVELY 18

FINAL THOUGHTS	19

DAY 6: 21

2 TIMOTHY 2:5 21

WHAT ARE THE RULES?	22
FINAL THOUGHTS:	24

DAY 7: 25

GALATIANS 5:7 25

QUESTIONING YOUR CHOICES	26
GETTING BACK UP	27
FINAL THOUGHTS	27

DAY 8: 29

PHILIPPIANS 3:14 29

IN YOUR OWN LIFE	30
IN THE WORLD	31
FINAL THOUGHTS	32

PART II: THE LAND 33

DAY 9: 33

RACING ON LAND 33

FEELING A CONNECTION WITH THE EARTH	34

DAY 10: 37

GENESIS 1:9-10 37

THE POWER OF HUMANITY	38
THE SMALLNESS OF PROBLEMS	38
FINAL THOUGHTS	39

DAY 11: 41

JEREMIAH 5:22 41

THE BOUNDARIES IN YOUR LIFE	42

THE SEA ALWAYS SUBSIDES.. 43
FINAL THOUGHTS 43

DAY 12: 45

PSALM 2:8 45

THE INHERITANCE OF THE EARTH 46
RESPECTING THE GIFT 47
FINAL THOUGHTS 47

DAY 13: 49

PROVERBS 27:23-24 49

PREPARING FOR THE FUTURE 51
FINAL THOUGHTS 51

DAY 14: 53

PROVERBS 12:10 53

THE RIGHTEOUS MAN 54
THE WICKED MAN 55
FINAL THOUGHTS 56

DAY 15: 57

PROVERBS 6:6-8 57

WORK HARD 58
TAKE CARE OF OTHERS 59
FINAL THOUGHTS 59

DAY 16: 61

PSALM 104:5 61

EVEN IN THE FACE OF STORMS 62
THE ROOTS OF A TREE 63
FINAL THOUGHTS 64

PART III: THE SEA 65

DAY 17: 65

RACING ON THE SEA 65

DAY 18: 67

JOB 26:10 67

THE STORMY SKY AND SEA 69
FINAL THOUGHTS 70

DAY 19: 71

MICAH 7:19 71

THE PAST AND THE SEA 72
ALL OF HUMANKIND 73
FINAL THOUGHTS 73

DAY 20: 75

ECCLESIASTES 1:6-7 75

RETURNING TO THE COURSE 76
FINAL THOUGHTS 77

DAY 21: 79

PROVERBS 20:5 79

WISDOM 80
FINAL THOUGHTS 81

DAY 22: 83

MARK 6:48-52 83

HUMAN CAPABILITY 84
WORKING TOGETHER 85
FINAL THOUGHTS 85

DAY 23: 87

MARK 6: 48-52 87

THE STORMS IN THE WORLD 88
FINAL THOUGHTS 89

DAY 24: 91

GENESIS 1:26 91

    WHAT IT MEANS TO BE A RULER... 92
    CARING FOR THE SEA 92
    FINAL THOUGHTS 93

PART IV: THE AIR 95

DAY 25: 95

RACING IN THE AIR 95

DAY 26: 97

PROVERBS 30:18-19 97

    THE EAGLE 98
    MANKIND 99
    FINAL THOUGHTS 99

DAY 27: 101

ISAIAH 40:31 101

    THE STRENGTHS OF THE EAGLE 102
    FINAL THOUGHTS 102

DAY 28: 103

REVELATION 9:2 103

    THE SUNLIGHT AND SMOKE 104
    DARKNESS IN THE WORLD 104
    FINAL THOUGHTS 105

DAY 29: 107

I CORINTHIANS 9:26 107

    SETTING A GOAL 108
    OTHERS BOXING AT THE AIR 108
    FINAL THOUGHTS 109

DAY 30: 111

MATTHEW 6:26 111

- The Birds in the Air 112
- You Will Be Taken Care Of 113
- Final Thoughts 113

DAY 31: 115

PROVERBS 27:8 115

- The Lesson of the Little Bird 116
- Final Thoughts 117

DAY 32: 119

PSALM 55:6 119

- The Difference in the Dove 120
- Final Thoughts 120

DAY 33: 121

EZEKIEL 31:3B-6 121

- The Tree 122
- Your Life 123
- Final Thoughts 123

DAY 34: 125

JAMES 4:14 125

- The Value of Life 126
- Final Thoughts 127

DAY 35: 129

JOB 12: 7-10 129

- Final Thoughts 131

DAY 36: 133

PSALM 103:11 133

Love Beyond End	134
Final Thoughts	134

PART V: THE RACE 135

DAY 37: 135

FINISHING THE RACE 135

DAY 38: 137

2 TIMOTHY 4:7 137

Setting Goals	138
Final Thoughts	138

DAY 39: 141

ACTS 20:24 141

The Value of All Mankind	142
Final Thoughts	142

DAY 40: 143

PHILIPPIANS 3:12-14 143

The Problem of Focusing on the Past	144
Final Thoughts	145

CONCLUSION 147

WORKS CITED 149

Introduction

What do you think when you consider your life? Do you see a vast opportunity in front of you? Do you see only the past and things you could have done differently? Do you only consider value or "success" in the things that you have, like a house, car, and toys?

There is so much more to life than this. It is a race. It is one with many legs to it as well. During the race of your life, you will run on the land, the sea, and the air. In that time, you will have to make numerous different choices that will extensively change your future.

When you focus on the right things in life, then you can run a better race and you can help out others who are struggling along their own journey.

For the next 40 days, we will spend time discussing each leg of the journey in detail. It doesn't matter what religion you are, if any one at all. It doesn't matter if you follow the Bible or not, there are things that can be learned from scriptures.

Are you ready to start running your race?

Read on…

Part I: The Race

Day 1:

1 Corinthians 9:24-27

Do you not know that in a race all runners run, but only one gets the prize? Run in such a way as to get the prize. Everyone who competes in the games goes into strict training. They do it to get a crown that will not last, but we do it to get a crown that will last forever. Therefore I do not run like someone running aimlessly; I do not fight like a boxer beating the air. No, I strike a blow to my body and make it my slave so that after I have preached to others, I myself will not be disqualified for the prize. (I Corinthians 9:24-27)

When you run the race, there are many different things that you must consider. The race of life goes well beyond just trying to attain something temporary like a crown or a trophy. You cannot look at it as a selfish chance to put another trophy on your mantle.

Instead, this race is about self-discipline, making the right decisions, and running toward a specific goal. For you, what does this mean?

Finding Your Goal

No race should be run without a goal. If you do run it in this way, then you will be running aimlessly in any direction that strikes your fancy. However, this is never the way to finish and it certainly isn't the way to win. Instead, you must consider your goals in life. What are they?

You should have two different sets of goals: those for you in the race and those that will help people around you. That's because we can only survive as a species if we help one another.

Training

Would you ever consider signing up for a marathon if you had not trained for it? Of course not! Most runners spend years preparing. You should not face the race of life without training either. If you do, then you will find it so much easier to make poor decisions, to choose the wrong path, and to lose your way. Training can include educating yourself so that you may achieve success in life, boosting your spirit through reading the Bible, and taking care of your body through exercise and healthy eating

Speaking to Others without Disqualification

Another thing you must consider about running life's race is the image that you are presenting to others. There is great pain, need, and loss in the world. Part of your job as a runner in the race is to help when you can. However, at the same time, you cannot disqualify yourself from reaching the finish line.

In other words, you must take care of yourself and continue growing and then you must share what you can with others.

Paul, the man who wrote this scripture, was a preacher. He describes part of his race as preaching to others so that they may learn from the teachings. He also states that he must preach to others in a way that he is constantly reminded of his own race. You must ask yourself, how can you help others through your own talents, abilities, and knowledge?

Final Thoughts

Now that you are beginning this 40 day race, let's take some time and establish a few things. Answer the following questions truthfully:

> Do I have a goal in this race or am I wandering aimlessly?
>
> If I have one, what is my goal?
>
> How am I training for this race?
>
> How am I helping others while staying on my path?
>
> Paul was a preacher, what are my gifts that I could use to help others?

Day 2:

Ecclesiastes 9:11-12

I have seen something else under the sun:

The race is not to the swift Or the battle to the strong Nor does food come to the wise

Or wealth to the brilliant Or favor to the learned; But time and chance happen to them all.

Moreover, no one knows when their hour will come:

As fish are caught in a cruel net, Or birds are taken in a snare, So people are trapped by evil times

That fall unexpectedly upon them. (Ecclesiastes 9:11-12)

Have you ever carefully designed your plans, laid out an idea, and then watched it fall completely apart? It happens to almost all of us, and it is the very thing this verse is referring to. It doesn't matter how strong, swift, or capable you are; this doesn't mean you will win a race.

Looking at Life

If you need a real-life example, take a look at Jim Thorpe. The  Native American competed in the Olympics and won numerous gold medals. He was considered the greatest athlete of the day. However, he lost all of his medals when researchers found out he had once played in a professional football league. That meant he was no longer an amateur and could not compete. Despite him being the swiftest and the strongest, he did not win the race. On the flip side of this, take a look at Mother Teresa. This small and seemingly very frail (obviously not the swiftest or strongest) was the recipient of the Nobel Peace Prize.

The Race in the World

Often, we believe that we can control everything. We attempt to force our wants and then we don't understand when it all falls apart. However, the world is flawed and life can be cruel. We are often like fish caught in a net. Taking a look at global issues like poverty will prove this point.

Part I: Day 2

The following facts are provided by www.DoSomething.org:

> "Nearly half of the world's population – more than 3 billion people – live on less than $2.50 a day. More than 1.3 billion people live in *extreme* poverty (less than $1.25 a day).
>
> 1 billion children worldwide are living in poverty. According to UNICEF, 22,000 children die each day due to poverty.
>
> 870 million people worldwide do not have enough food to eat. (11 Facts About Global Poverty)

We are often so busy running the race of our own lives that we seem to forget those others who are caught in snares. They do not have a way out of those traps and it requires others to realize that they can help while running their race.

According to the World Food Program, "The poor are hungry and their hunger traps them in poverty. Hunger is the number one cause of death in the world, killing more than HIV/AIDS, malaria, and tuberculosis combined." (11 Facts About Global Poverty)

Let's look at a few more facts provided by the World Health Organization:

> Children in low-income countries are 16 times more likely to die before reaching the age of five than children in high-income countries.
>
> Almost half of the countries surveyed have access to less than half the essential medicines they need for basic health care in the public sector.
>
> Even though almost 1.9 billion people have gained access to improved sanitation facilities since 1990, global coverage is currently estimated at just 64%, leaving one third of the global population (2.5 billion people) without access. (Organization, 2013)

If we are to survive as a species (mankind), we cannot run the race separately. Just as this Bible verse says, the race doesn't necessarily go to the strongest. All types are needed.

Final Thoughts

Take a moment and think of the race you have been running and then answer the following questions:

> Who have I been running the race for, me or all of mankind?
>
> Have I been doing anything to help others?
>
> What could I do that might help others who are caught in the net like a fish?

Day 3:

John 16:33

I have told you these things, so that in me you may have peace. In the world, you will have trouble. But take heart! I have overcome the world. (John 16:33)

The world is flawed. There is always trouble in it and that trouble affects us all in some way or another. It doesn't matter how nice of a house you live in or what type of car you drive, you could be affected by the numerous problems that surround you, like crime, sickness, and loss.

According to Nation Master...

> The eighth United Nations Survey on Crime Trends and the Operations of Criminal Justice Systems indicates that in one year, there were 11,877,218 total crimes in the United States alone. This was the highest in the 42 countries surveyed.
>
> In Turkey, there were 13,424 murders in one year. This was the highest of the countries surveyed.
>
> France had the highest rate of rapes at a total of 10,277 in one year. (Nations Compared)

There is crime in the world. There is hunger. There is suffering.

Personal Challenges

In your own life, there are bound to be personal challenges. You may have family troubles, stress at work, relationship issues, health concerns, or something else. We all face personal challenges in our lives. It is just a part of living.

You don't have to feel alone. Instead, just remember that the people around you are facing their own challenges as well. Most importantly, when you face your next challenge, you must remember that it can be overcome.

Collective Challenges

It's very easy to get wrapped up in your own problems. We are all guilty of it from time to time. However, you do have to consider that everyone else is dealing with problems of their own.

More than this, all of mankind as a collective has challenges, like the high crime rate, lack of fresh water, lack of food, poverty, drug use, and more. By remembering that everyone has problems and challenges, it becomes easier for each of us to recognize the need to work together for the good of all.

Final Thoughts

Challenges are all around us. We all face them. Sometimes they are bigger than others. Think about these questions:

> When was the last time you faced a personal challenge? How did you overcome it?
>
> Try to think of some of the collective challenges you see in your community. What can you do to make a change for the better?
>
> Are you facing personal challenges right now? Do you know how to overcome them?

Finally, the next time you have trouble with someone else, remind yourself that they may be dealing with their own challenges and they deserve kindness. You don't know when your kind word may be enough of a boost so that they can overcome their challenges and move on.

Day 4:

2 Timothy 1:7

For the Spirit God gave us does not make us timid, but gives us power, love, and self-discipline. (2 Timothy 1:7)

Yes, the world is full of troubles, and the race can be difficult at times. However, as a human being, you have power within you. If you are timid and step aside, you will never finish that race. Instead, you will be left in the dust.

While that power is within us all, we often forget it. It is so easy to just throw up your hands and walk away from a difficult situation, but that isn't always the right answer. In fact, being timid is never the right answer.

Power Over Timidity

You do have power over any timidity you may feel. When you find yourself in a situation where it seems to be easier to just back down, you have to be strong. Additionally, when mankind unites, that power becomes even stronger. It is most certainly the answer to surviving as a species.

Love

We are given the ability to love for a very good reason. That's because within love, there lies power. What do I mean?

- When you have the love of a family, you feel strong enough to accomplish your dreams.

- When you have the love of someone else, you feel less lonely and perhaps more complete.

- When you love your own children, you have the ability to do anything for them.

In other words, the very notion of love is strength and power. It is essential to human beings just as much as oxygen or food.

Self-Discipline

Imagine where you would be in life without self-discipline. What if you ate that doughnut whenever you wanted or didn't ever get up when the alarm went off? You certainly wouldn't be successful. You may have numerous health problems. And you may not have the want to or will to help others. We are given self-discipline because we need it to survive.

Final Thoughts

Now that you have thought a little more about your own power through love and self-discipline, it is time to ask those questions:

> Have you allowed timidity to take control? How will you get your power back?
>
> In what situation has self-discipline been important in your life?
>
> How has love helped you gain the power you needed in a situation?

Day 5:

Psalm 119:71

It was good for me to be afflicted

So that I might learn your decrees. (Psalm 119:71)

There is a hard lesson to learn in those two lines. However, it is so very important in the race of life. Think about this little scenario:

Say you are in a real foot race. Up until the very last few feet before the finish line, you never stepped on a rock, stumbled, or tripped. Then, when you are just steps away, your foot trips on a small stone in the way. Because you have never encountered it before, you stumble and fall. You end up losing the race.

Now, think about this. You are running that same race. Several times along the way, you stumbled over a rock or something else that got in your way. You learned how to deal with those little speed bumps. By the time you get near the finish line, they are not that much of an issue. Yes, you stumble over that small stone, but this time, you keep your footing and win the race.

What is the lesson that can be learned here?

If we never encounter obstacles, we never have a chance to learn from them.

Learning from Individual Troubles

For a moment, think back to some obstacle you have faced in your life. It could be related to work, your home life, your health, or anything else. Just think of one thing. Now, think about what you would do if you encountered that same problem now. You would know much more about how to handle it because you have dealt with it before.

Individual obstacles are required because they give us the experience and knowledge we need to make smarter, better decisions in our lives.

Learning from Troubles Collectively

Mankind also must learn from troubles as a whole. It is the only way to continue existence. There are plenty of good examples of how well it can work when we do. For example, the World Health

Organization was formed so that we can all work together to eradicate disease, starvation, and other problems. The organization reports that since 1990, the number of people who are without fresh drinking water has been cut almost in half.

We can learn from our obstacles as well. In fact, when you deal with trouble of your own, you may be tempted to keep this information to yourself. You may think that if you share your issues, then someone will consider you weak. However, you actually owe it to mankind to speak out about your obstacles. Perhaps someone else will hear your story and will be able to overcome their troubles because of it.

Final Thoughts

Think of an obstacle you have faced. How did you overcome it? What did you learn from it?

Do you spend time complaining about troubles or do you use them as learning tools?

What is one worldwide obstacle that you could help overcome?

Day 6:

2 Timothy 2:5

Similarly, anyone who competes as an athlete does not receive the victor's crown except by competing according to the rules. (2 Timothy 2:5)

Lance Armstrong is considered one of the greatest athletes of the modern day. He won seven Tour de France titles and is also known for numerous different charitable contributions. He seemed to be a golden child of the athletic world. Then, something happened. He tested positive for performance-enhancing drugs (steroids). Because he broke the rules, he was stripped of all seven awards and he was banned for life in the cycling tournament.

He lost everything and now his legacy will be forever stained with this issue. He didn't follow the rules and this came back to haunt him.

This is an important lesson that you should remember for your own life. To win the race, you have to follow the rules.

What Are the Rules?

It's hard to sit down and list out very specific rules for the race of life. Different organizations, groups, entities, and religions all have their own set. If you follow the Bible, then the rules are laid out for you in black and white. You could also refer to the rules of life as those set forth by the law. No matter how you look at it, there are rules and you have to follow them.

Some of them are obvious:

- Murder is wrong

- Illegal drugs will bring consequences

- Hurting someone else just to promote yourself is a bad thing

Some things can be a bit in the gray area, too. However, the best choice you could make is to follow your conscience. Before you do something, try to consider whether it will help or hinder, whether it will harm or lift up.

Following the rules also applies to the whole world and all of mankind. If we break the rules as a collective, it has detrimental effects on us all. Just think about World War II. A whole group broke the rules and committed mass genocide. The result was a war that affected almost every country in the world. It brought about numerous deaths, the dropping of two atomic bombs, and a great deal of pain.

We should all strive to follow the rules of life because it is the only way to win the race.

Final Thoughts:

Ask yourself the following questions. They can help you better see the importance of rules in your own life.

> Think of a time when you broke the rules. Maybe it was at school or at home. Perhaps it was in childhood or adulthood. Just consider it and then think about the consequences you had to deal with for breaking the rules. They set you back in some way in the race – what was that way?
>
> Do you think that the world society as a collective is following the rules very well? Why or why not?

Day 7:

Galatians 5:7

Y ou are running a good race. Who cut in on you to keep you from obeying the truth? (Galatians 5:7)

If you are running a race and you are in the lead, what would happen if someone came along, perhaps another runner, and tripped you up? You would probably lose the race and you would most definitely lose your lead.

The race of life is very similar to this. There are plenty of obstacles in the way. There are other runners (people), rocks (things), and your own shoes (your own emotions and mind) that can cause you to trip if you allow them to.

Questioning Your Choices

Every day, you could face things that will get in your way and keep you from running a good race. You may deal with situations when it is very hard to follow the rules we talked about yesterday. However, you have to make the decision to continue running a good race. It is the only way to win.

How can you ensure this? Question your choices. Ask yourself:

- Is someone leading me in the wrong direction?
- Am I allowing something to get in my way?
- Am I keeping to the rules I know to be true for me?

Every day, you must attempt to answer those questions. After all, the race of life doesn't stop.

Getting Back Up

The reality is, there will be times when you get tripped up. It happens to everyone. That doesn't mean the race is over just because you lost sight of the truth for a while. Instead, it means you get up, dust yourself off, and start running again.

Stephen King, arguably one of the best modern authors, was rejected dozens of times for his novel, *Carrie*. What if he had given up at the first rejection and never kept running the race? Obviously, those publishers were the ones who were attempting to keep him from his truth, which turned out to be that he could be a bestselling author. Because King got back up, he has gone on to write dozens of bestselling books and short stories.

Final Thoughts

Do you feel like anything or anyone has been stepping in your way and withholding you from truth?

What can you do to remove those stumbling blocks from your path?

Do you see anything that is withholding the whole of mankind from the truth? If so, what is it?

Day 8:

Philippians 3:14

I press on toward the goal to win the prize… (Philippians 3:14)

Just a few simple words can have so much power. It is amazing what you can learn from a sentence. Often, you will encounter bad things in your life. They may be a struggle. You may even find yourself thinking it would be best just to throw your hands in the air and give up. However, if every racer did that, then no one would ever win. Not only would choices like this be detrimental for you, they would be detrimental to society.

You must press onward toward the goal no matter how hard the race gets and no matter how many stumbling blocks you may encounter. If you don't, you will never win the prize of a good life.

In Your Own Life

This is the final chapter in the first section of this devotional. Tomorrow, we will start talking about the race of life and land. To finish things up with this section, it is time to spend some time reflecting on your own life.

Be completely honest with yourself. No one else is listening or judging you.

- Are you pressing toward the goal?
- At your job?
- At home?
- With friends?
- With other activities?
- Are there ways you could improve your own race?
- Has there been a time when you just wanted to give up because something seemed to be too hard? What kept you going?

Truly reflect on the race you have been running and determine if there are ways you could race faster. A foot racer is always looking to improve through training, new gear, and proper nutrition. You have to look for ways to improve as well.

Part I: Day 8 ■ 31

In the World

Running the race of life isn't just about you, either. As a species, mankind must always be pressing toward the goal. Obviously, there are many goals in this case, like solving poverty, eradicating disease, and eliminating crime.

While you are working toward your goals in your own life, try to think of ways you could help to improve the world as a species as well.

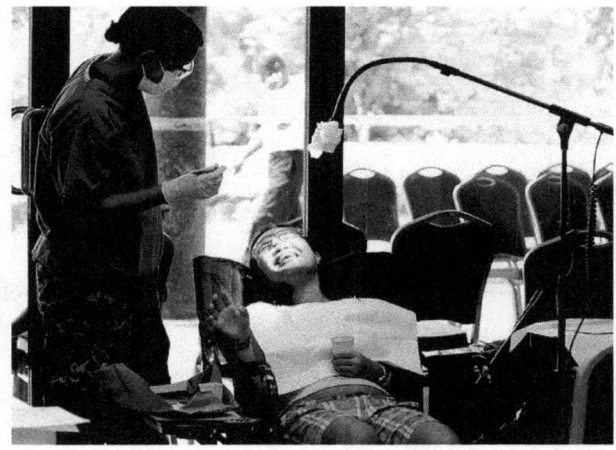

- What are some of the goals for mankind that you can think of?

- Are there things you could do to help others continue running the race?

- Think of someone important in your life. Think of a way you could help them press forward, especially if they are encountering stumbling blocks.

- Think of a complete stranger. Now, think of ways you could help them press forward in their own race.

Final Thoughts

Pressing toward the goal always has to be the one thing we work hardest at. It applies to so many parts of your life, too – work, play, personal relationships, family, hobbies, and everything else.

From this section of the devotional, let's review some key things to take away:

> There will be things standing in your way in the race.
>
> Troubles occur for everyone.
>
> There is trouble for the whole world and all of mankind.
>
> It is your responsibility to set your goals and help all of mankind run the race.
>
> You have power within you to fight any battle.
>
> You have to learn your own truths so that you may follow the rules.
>
> At all times, press forward for you and for mankind to win the race.

Part II: The Land

Day 9:

Racing on Land

Often, in championship races, the participants must take on different legs of the journey. They may be required to run or bike on land, swim in the water, or even sail in boats with the wind pushing the sails.

The race of life could be broken up into several categories as well. We have already discussed the race overall. Now, let's look at your life and the life of all mankind based on land. The earth is so important. Because of it, we are living. We have a place to:

- Plant vegetables and fruits for our sustenance

- Dig for water so that we may be hydrated

- Build our houses so that we may have shelter from storms

- Raise livestock and animals so that we may have food and companionship

The earth does even more than that.

Feeling a Connection with the Earth

Have you ever been to the beach? Have you stood with your bare toes in the sand, just enjoying the feel of your skin against the earth? Maybe it wasn't the beach for you. Perhaps you stood barefoot in the grass at a park or just walked outside of your home. No matter what, there is something so comforting and grounding about feeling something solid and definite beneath your feet.

The land is a part of your life and it is a definite part of the race of life. This holds true for you and for every other person who walks this earth.

On the next page, we will move on to Day 10. Are you ready to learn how you can improve your race on land? Ask any runner and they will say that this is most certainly an important leg of their journey, whether they are on foot, on a bicycle, or riding in a vehicle. It is also true of the race in life. You can learn different things that will ensure you make the most of your own race on land.

Are you ready?

Day 10:

Genesis 1:9-10

And God said, 'Let the water under the sky be gathered to one place, and let the dry ground appear.' And it was so. God called the dry ground 'land,' and the gathered waters he called 'seas.'

And God saw that it was good. (Genesis 1:9-10)

Have you ever looked into the history of the earth? Some people may find it a little dry or "boring," but in many ways, it is extremely fascinating. Many years ago, the earth was just a spherical ball floating through space. Then, there was a great upheaval. Land began to form and the water separated.

There are maps that show how all of the land was once one piece. It was broken up into what we now call the continents. When the land began to push together, mountains began to form. Where it split apart, oceans were formed. It took years for this to happen (in human terms) and the result is the earth we know today.

The Power of Humanity

Now, think of your own life in relation to this great creation of the earth. You may at first feel a little insignificant, but instead, you are extremely important. All of these events that formed the land you walk on happened so that you would have a place to live. You, as a human, are just that important. So too is every other human on the earth.

Since humanity is so powerful and since the earth was formed just so we would have a place to live and farm and play, we have the power to stop the troubles of the species. It only takes an effort in your race to make a change. If we all make that effort, then we can see a drastic difference.

The Smallness of Problems

It is easy to get wrapped up in our own problems. We tend to think that we are the only ones suffering. However, everyone on the planet has troubles that they must face on a regular basis. Sometimes, those problems are larger than at other times.

However, when you think of the enormity of the formation of the earth, you will realize that any problems you may face are actually extremely small.

There is nothing that you cannot overcome. Whenever you feel like you are drowning in troubles, simply remember the vast earth. Remember how it was formed. Remember that it was formed for you.

Final Thoughts

Now that you have started thinking about the earth and the land, take the time to ponder a few things:

> Do you understand what type of power you hold in your hands to change things?
>
> How could you use that power to help others and make a difference in the race of life for mankind?
>
> Take the time and consider any problems that may be bothering you. Think about how small they are in the vast enormity of the world. They seem a little less daunting, don't they?

Day 11:

Jeremiah 5:22

Should you not fear me?' declares the Lord. 'Should you not tremble in my presence?

I made the sand a boundary for the sea, An everlasting barrier it cannot cross.

The waves may roll, but they cannot prevail; They may roar but they cannot cross it.' (Jeremiah 5:22)

There is an interesting thing about the land and the sea. If you look at the land, you will notice that in many places, it is actually lower than the sea. Places like southern Louisiana are below sea level. How is this possible? When you really start to think about it, you will realize that it takes a great power to withhold the oceans from overtaking the land. Because of that force, we have a place to live, grow, enjoy our time, and farm for sustenance.

While there are times when the sea has overtaken the earth (flood and hurricanes), it always subsides and it always goes back to its boundaries that can never be crossed.

The Boundaries in Your Life

In many ways, the boundary between the land and the sea could be a symbol of your own life.

On the land, you have everything you need to survive and even be happy. You have food, shelter, clothing, friends, family, and so much more. On the land, you feel safe and strong.

From the land, you can see the sea. You see the choppy waves and how they can toss ships about or even damage them. However, you are safe on land because it is stable and strong.

There are times when that sea will overtake the land where you stand, though. It happens just as a hurricane occasionally comes along and floods parts of the earth. When this happens, you will experience stormy times in your own life. You may have trouble at work or you may have a relationship problem. The sea can be strong and it could be so stormy that it knocks you down.

The Sea Always Subsides

However, you do always need to remember one very important thing: The sea always subsides, even after a terrible storm. This is the same for your life. When you experience trouble in your life, no matter how hard it seems to knock you down, it will subside. The struggles will always clear up and you will be able to enjoy your strong footing on the land once again.

All that you have to do is be patient and stand strong when the water seems to be rising.

Final Thoughts

The land is much stronger than you could ever even imagine. Even when it is ravaged by the oceans and storms, it remains stalwart. It gives us shelter. It gives us food. It is always there and boundaries always remain between the land and the water. The water always subsides and we always have dry land to stand on. Think of this symbolism in your own life.

How does this apply to your own life?

Have you ever noticed that while problems may seem so big, they always subside just as the sea does from the shore?

Think about all of humanity. While there always seem to be problems somewhere in the world, when all humans work together, they have a capability to solve those problems and enjoy the boundaries between land and sea. What times in your life have you seen mankind work together to weather the stormy oceans?

Day 12:

Psalm 2:8

Ask me, and I will make the nations your inheritance, The ends of the earth your possession. (Psalms 2:8)

When you are given an inheritance, what should you do with it? Should you waste it away and find yourself broke just a few months later? Wouldn't it be better if you were smart with your newfound money? Obviously, you could do so much with an inheritance. You could easily store

some of it away and ensure you have money that you may need in the future. You could use it to ensure you don't have to deal with debt or other problems.

An inheritance is a great gift, and it would have been given to you by someone who thought so highly of you that they wanted to ensure you were financially secure.

The Inheritance of the Earth

The land, the earth, is like an inheritance to all of humankind. It is a gift that we have been given, and it is one that we should take care of properly. If we just squander it away, what will we be left with in the future?

Part of your race of life on land means caring for that land specifically. If you don't, then it could suffer damage and it may not be available for others to race on in future.

That means you should take the time to look after the land in any way that you can, like:

- Choosing to recycle instead of sending more things to the dump.
- Choosing to use biodegradable products for cleaning and other chemicals.
- Making an effort to protect forests and wildlife.
- Avoiding contributing to a problem by choosing not to litter and by choosing to properly dispose of chemicals.

Anything you can do to ensure the land is taken care of and not abused will be a big step toward ensuring that the earth will still be available for generations after you to run their race on.

Respecting the Gift

Essentially, the earth is a gift so that we humans have a place to live, work, and play. We must respect that gift.

Just imagine if the land became barren, empty, and windswept. There would be no place to live, no place to enjoy nature, and no place to grow food. It certainly would be a difficult way to live and definitely would not be the best way to run the human race.

Renewable energy sources by type:

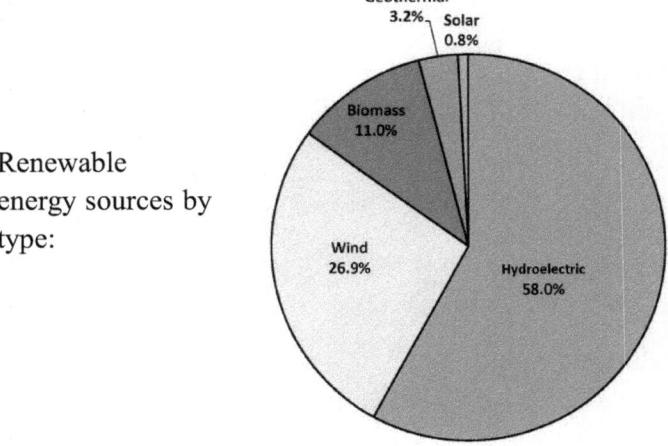

Final Thoughts

Now that you begin thinking about the land as a gift to you or as an inheritance, you have to start asking a few questions:

> How well have you been taking care of your inheritance?

Are there ways you could improve your gift by caring for it and nurturing it in the future?

Day 13:

Proverbs 27:23-24

Be sure you know the condition of your flocks,

Give careful attention to your herds;

For riches do not endure forever,

And a crown is not secure for all generations.

(Proverbs 27:23-24)

Part of the race on land has to do with the animals and plants around you. Without them, you would not be able to survive. After all, the livestock like sheep, cows, goats, and other herds provide you with sustenance. The plants provide you with fruits and vegetables. This is the first lesson to glean from the verse.

If you don't take care of the things around you, you won't necessarily have them in the future. We often are very shortsighted human beings and we don't look past the here and now. However, if you don't take the time to consider the future, then the coming years could be very bleak.

Think about it this way. If you talked to a cattle herder, would he say that it is ok to neglect his cattle? Would he stop feeding them, leave them out in the bad weather, or refuse them water?

Of course not. After all, the herd is how the herder makes a living. If the cattle become emaciated or sick or even die, he will have no livestock to sell. You have to live in the same manner, protecting all of the elements on the earth because the land does provide for you.

Think of this real-life example when it comes to cattle. The cows were not well taken care of in some countries and the result was an outbreak of "mad cow disease" in Europe. Quite a few people became sick. Now, people have to be extremely careful where they buy their foods. If we don't take care of the animals, this could harm us extensively. It all works in sort of a circle.

Preparing for the Future

The second thing you can learn from this verse is to think about the future. The verse says "riches do not endure forever, and a crown is not secure for all generations." What does this mean?

You don't know what could happen in the future. You may not be financially stable or secure. Your children and their children may not have the security you would like. You have no way of knowing what may happen down the road. Things like money and belongings don't last forever. They could be taken away in the blink of an eye by a house fire, burglary, bankruptcy, and so many other things.

Instead of putting so much value on things that could be taken away, you must remember the value of the land and care for it as well.

At the same time, you must always prepare for the future. That means taking steps to ensure you are able to care for yourself and for your family if you don't always have money and belongings.

Final Thoughts

Obviously, these days, you probably don't happen to have a flock or herd of cattle unless you are actually a farmer. However, this verse can certainly still be applicable when it comes to your race of life on the land.

> How well have you been "caring for the flock"? Are you taking care of the earth the best you can?

Have you thought about the future and what you would do if you lost belongings and money?

Do you put too much importance on things instead of on what actually lasts, like the earth?

Have you considered how you could ensure your children and grandchildren are protected if you lose "the crown"? (Lose money or belongings)

Have you considered just how important of a role the land plays in your life and your own race?

Have you considered just how important the livestock and animals are to the land and how important they are to humankind?

Day 14:

Proverbs 12:10

The righteous care for the needs of their animals,

But the kindest acts of the wicked are cruel.

(Proverbs 12:10)

If you talk to a psychologist, they will probably agree. When

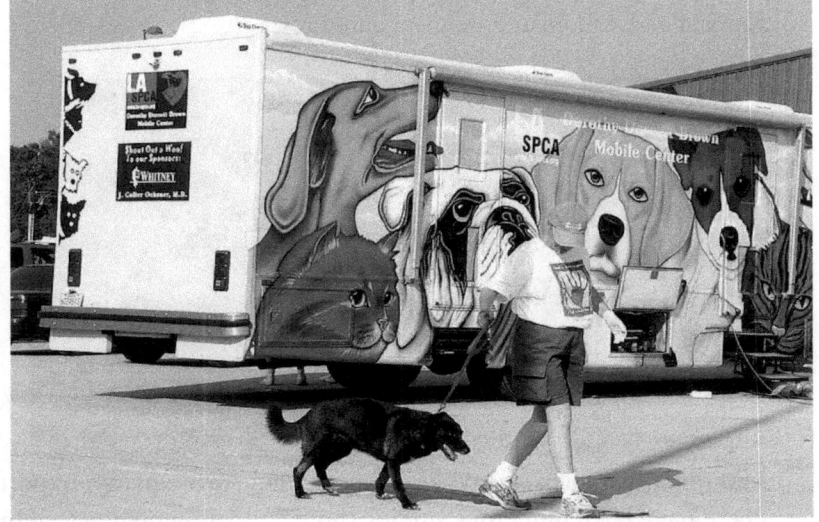

someone is cruel to animals, they are more likely to be cruel to other humans. There have been numerous examples of this. So often, well-known serial killers began their path of destruction by harming cats and dogs. That's what this verse is referring to. The people who are good, pure, and kind are also good to the animals even if they don't have pets. The people who are wicked, cold-hearted, and just plain mean, even at their kindest, are still cruel.

What does this mean for you and your race in life? Let's explore the verse a little more thoroughly.

The Righteous Man

Another way to say that would be "a good person." The verse states that the good person will regard the life of the animals. In other words, he will take care of them, ensure they are safe, and make sure they are preserved. The good man will provide food for animals, choose not to overwork them, and ensure they have health care if they become sick.

The reason for this is quite simple. Animals, like livestock are needed. They are an important part of our human race. They are often our livelihood. A good person will recognize the value in the animals and will ensure they are cared for.

Additionally, when it comes to pets, they are equally important. There have been numerous studies showing that owning pets actually has numerous different health benefits. These studies indicate having cats and dogs will:

- Lower blood pressure
- Extend life
- Ease depression

Numerous groups use therapy dogs to visit people in the hospital because they have realized that animals can help ease suffering and even bring an end to illness to some degree. These animals are valuable to our race on land, and a good person will take care of them.

The Wicked Man

If the tenderest mercies of the wicked are cruel, then what does this mean when they are actually trying to be cruel? There are many examples of this. That's why people are being tortured right this very moment somewhere in the world. That's why maniacs commit mass genocide. That's why horrors like the attack on the World Trade Center happen. It's why there are drug lords controlling and starving innocent people in Africa and South America.

The most merciful actions of the wicked still remain cruel, so it is vital that we understand how to protect ourselves and others (as well as the animals of the land) from that cruelty.

Final Thoughts

There is only one final thought to discuss here:

Do you understand the value of the animals on the earth? Do you care for them when you can? Do you avoid anything that could be construed as wicked? They do matter in your own personal race of life, so you do need to ensure you are respecting them at all times.

Day 15:

Proverbs 6:6-8

G o to the ant, you sluggard; Consider its ways and be wise!

It has no commander, No overseer or ruler,

Yet it stores provisions in the summer And gathers food at harvest. (Proverbs 6:6-8)

There is so much that we can learn from the land as well. There are numerous different lessons that you can glean even from the smallest of the creatures that walk the earth.

Just take a look at the ant. This tiny little bug is one of the hardest workers on the whole planet. It works tirelessly to build hills, provide food, and prevent damage or attack. The ant is so strong it can lift hundreds of times its own body weight as well. A creature like this can offer so many lessons to us as humans.

Work Hard

The ant is a hard little worker, and the tiny insect doesn't even have a boss or parents telling it what to do. Instead, it knows what needs to be done and it does it.

This is how you must lead your own life. You shouldn't constantly be dependent on someone else to always tell you what to do. Instead, you should recognize what should be done and then take action.

Like the ant, you should work hard (that doesn't mean overwork yourself. Even ants take breaks). You should ensure that you are doing everything you can to make smart decisions in every aspect of your life.

Take Care of Others

The ant doesn't just work to care for itself. Instead, it brings food for the whole colony. It builds a strong mound to protect against storms, predators, and other ants. It ensures that the colony will go on and survive. This is something else you need to learn from the ant.

We shouldn't just worry about ourselves. We should worry about all of mankind. We should work to provide a better world for them, and that means helping to provide necessities to the underprivileged. It means working toward better disease control and better food and water sources as well.

Final Thoughts

Take some time to think about that little ant and compare your own life choices to it. Think about how you are running the race on land.

> Are you working like an ant or do you depend on others to make decisions for you?
>
> Do you help out by working for the whole of humankind or just yourself?
>
> Think of the last time you saw a homeless person on the street. Did you ignore their situation and walk by or did you stop to see if you could help? Once you answer that question, think about whether or not you made the right decision.

Day 16:

Psalm 104:5

H e set the earth on its foundations;
It can never be moved.
(Psam 104:5)

The land that you race on, it cannot be moved. It has incredibly strong foundations and the land itself may be shaken or ravaged, but nothing can destroy those foundations beneath it. What a wonderful thing to think about!

No matter where you go in life and no matter what part of the race you encounter, you will always have the land beneath your feet. You can have hope in this fact that the earth and the land are much bigger than anything you may encounter or go through. This can be a great comfort when you are facing a time of struggle.

Even in the Face of Storms

Even when strong hurricanes shake the coastal states or when earthquakes literally cause the land to move, it will still remain solid. The earth has been here for millions of years and it has withstood a variety of different storms even of great strength.

You can learn something about this for your race of life as well. Like the land, you must recognize your own capabilities to weather storms. You will be able to get through almost anything as long as you keep your foundations strong. How can you do this?

- Remember the importance of family and relationships.
- Build a support system that will help you remain strong in the face of storms.
- Know the importance of having values. Knowing what you stand for makes it easier to stand strong.

Part II: Day 16 ■ 63

- Know that there is a reason you are on this earth.
- Think about your reason for being here often. It roots you to the earth.

When you build up strong foundations, then you will find it easier to weather any storm that may be thrown your way. That's because the strongest of foundations cannot be shaken. However, a person with no foundations can much more easily be damaged by the storms.

The Roots of a Tree

Every day, you drive or walk or ride by trees that have actually weathered numerous storms. Those trees often stay strong even in the high winds or torrential downpours. They bend with the wind and they may lose a branch or two, but they do not give in.

What keeps the trees so strong? The land. They have deep roots in the earth, and those roots provide sustenance as well as strength. If the tree didn't have those deep roots, it would be destroyed by the first storm that came along.

In your own life, you must also be like the tree. Know that there is strength in the land and draw from it. You can get everything you need – food, water, building materials, clothing materials – all from the land. Always remember the strength that the land can offer in your race.

Final Thoughts

This is the last day discussing the race on land, so for final thoughts, take the time and consider what you may have gleaned from these devotionals.

> What day stood out the most to you and spoke to you the deepest?
>
> What did you learn from that day?
>
> Does this change your perspective on the importance of land for all mankind?

Part III: The Sea

Day 17:

Racing on the Sea

The next leg of the race is on the sea. You already know that the sea can be stormy sometimes. The waves may roll and toss you about. Because this part of life's race can be so difficult, you most certainly do need a little guidance along your way. This way, you will always know how to make the best decisions.

When racers in the water get started, they have guidance. Swimmers will have lanes that are clearly marked so that they can follow them. Sailors in races and regattas will have maps and other charts so that they will know where to go. You need guidance in your race of life, too.

Are you ready to learn more about the sea? Then, let's move on to Day 18.

Day 18:

Job 26:10

He marks out the horizon on the face of the waters

For a boundary between light and darkness.

(Job 26:10)

When you stand on the beach and look out at the horizon, you will see that there is a distinct line between where the waters stop and where the sky begins. It is certainly understandable that cultures many years ago thought the earth was flat. It certainly looks that way when you stand at the edge of the ocean.

If you visit the east coast, you can watch the sun rise from the horizon. If you are at the west coast, then you can watch it set. In either case, it seems that the horizon works as more than just a bounding line. It is also the moment from dark to light, from night to day.

In your life, there is a definite boundary between light and darkness, good and evil, wrong and right. Just like the line between the sea and the sky where the sun rises and sets, you have a line in your life.

Think of it as a guideline. Think of it as your conscience. You can even call it your inner compass. No matter what you may call it, this line helps you determine if an action will be right or wrong. There is a very good reason why you have this boundary. It helps you make decisions every day. Additionally, imagine if you didn't have it...that no one had it. The world would be a very different place.

The Stormy Sky and Sea

Sometimes, you can stand at the ocean and the sky is so stormy and the sea so choppy that it is rather hard to see the horizon clearly. Things become blurred and you may not even be sure if there is a sun behind the clouds.

You have those moments in your life too when the boundary may be blurred. You may have to make decisions when you aren't completely sure what the right choice would be. It can be very hard to make a decision in that case. After all, you may be very concerned you will make the wrong choice. What do you do?

- Try to think about the possible outcome of each of your choices. Consider what could happen in the future based on the decision you make.

- Think about whether or not someone will be injured by the decision you make. Obviously, if one of the choices causes harm, then it would be the wrong one in most cases.

Even when the lines are blurred, you can still make the right decision. That's because even when there are clouds in the sky and choppy seas, there is a horizon hidden by the blurriness. There is a boundary hidden in the difficult decision as well. You can make the right choice if you just take the time to consider your avenues.

Final Thoughts

There will be times in your life when you can see the horizon clearly and then there will be other times when you won't be able to see that line so clearly.

> Think of a time you had to make a decision when the lines were blurry. What choice did you make and why?

> Have you ever made the wrong choice? What kind of consequences did this bring to you?

Day 19:

Micah 7:19

Y ou will again have compassion on us;

You will tread our sins underfoot

And hurl all our iniquities into the depths of the sea.

(Micah 7:19)

There are places in the sea that are so deep that we cannot explore them very much. There are also places where the sea is so deep that

the sunlight cannot filter through and the waters are completely black. Often, people refer to the oceans as the vast undiscovered territory, and that is certainly true for many reasons. Humans continue to try to explore and the sea is one of the last places where new species of wildlife are discovered.

It can be so easy whenever you make a mistake or wrong decision to focus on that wrong choice and make yourself miserable. Most people have a strong conscience, and making the wrong decision, especially if it injures someone else, can be detrimental in many ways. You may find yourself dwelling on the past, rethinking your choices, and imagining what would have been different if you made a different decision. It could make you miserable.

The Past and the Sea

Take a moment and really think about it. When you dwell on the decisions of your past, what are you doing with your present? You are spending too much time worrying about something that cannot change. The past is exactly what it is. It is the past. You can't go back and change your decision. All you can do is make better choices in the present and the future. By dwelling on the past, you are not making those right decisions now.

Whenever you start worrying over a bad decision or choice you have made, imagine this little scenario:

Imagine sailing on a big ship out to the deepest parts of the ocean. When you look over the rail, you see the churning waters that disappear into a great darkness. Now, imagine taking that wrong choice or decision from the past and then throwing it overboard so that it drops down and cannot be seen again.

Once that choice or decision has sunken to the depths of the ocean, you certainly cannot worry over it again. It will be gone. You can only focus on the present and making right decisions now.

All of Humankind

As a collective species, humankind is very strong. We have survived so many disasters and catastrophes. We have seen the best and the worst that the world has to offer. We have made wrong decisions, questionable decisions, and the best decisions. Mankind cannot spend too much time dwelling on the past, especially when there are so many problems that need to be dealt with in the now. Focusing on a wrong decision from years ago will certainly not ensure that hunger, drought, wars, and other problems aren't being addressed.

We must toss our problems into the depths of the dark sea, so to speak. Then, we can only focus on the present.

Final Thoughts

Dwelling doesn't accomplish anything, especially when it hinders you from making the right choices now.

> What is a bad choice you have made in the past? Are you dwelling on it?
>
> Do you think that you are spending too much time worrying about the past?
>
> Think about all of humanity. Do you think that we are dwelling on the past as a species?

Day 20:

Ecclesiastes 1:6-7

The wind blows to the south And turns to the north; Round and round it goes, Ever returning on its course. All streams flow into the sea, Yet the sea is never full. To the place the streams come from, There they return again.

(Ecclesiastes 1:6-7)

Every single day, rivers flow in countries all over the world. They all empty into the ocean or the sea. If you think about this, you would

think that the oceans would continually rise. After all, that is a lot of water flowing into it. Why doesn't it rise? The earth has a very unique system that ensures this will never happen. The waters flow into the seas.

Then, a scientific process of evaporation and cloud formation takes place over the oceans. Those clouds travel to the land and bring rain. Not only does rain nourish the land, provide living beings with water, and ensure the crops will grow, but it also flows to the rivers that then send their water out to the sea.

No matter what else happens on the earth, no matter what mankind does as a whole, no matter any disaster or good thing that occurs, the rivers will always empty to the sea, the seas will always provide rain, and the rivers will always draw in the rain and move it to the sea again. It's a vast process or cycle that is extremely important to our livelihood.

Returning to the Course

There are times when this cycle is interrupted to some extent. Sometimes, the land goes through a drought and rivers may even dry up. However, something happens. No matter how long the interruptions last, the process will always return back to normal. The cycle continues even in the face of barriers or interruptions.

Just as the rivers and the seas always return to the course, your life will always return to the course even when it seems to be interrupted from time to time.

There are many different times when life as a whole for all of humankind seems to be interrupted from its course:

- Wars
- Famines
- Immense government debts
- Disagreements between countries

However, all of these things do come to an end. When they do, the proper course of humankind is restored. There are many reasons why we exist, and you may find some reasons more important than the others. In any case, even when these reasons seem to have become derailed, they will come back just as the rivers and the seas will continue their proper process even after a storm.

The river rights itself. That means mankind has to right itself as well. In other words, it is our duty to ensure we find our way back to the proper course even when bad things have happened that seem to negatively affect all of us.

Final Thoughts

It's easy to understand the cycle of life when you look at the rivers and the seas. They always work together to create a process required for us to even survive.

> Think of a time in your life when your purpose was derailed. Then, think about this: what happened? Did you get back on course?

> Think of an event that has derailed humanity. Is that event still going on or have we found our way back to our proper purpose?

Is there some way you could help right now with a problem that seems to be pushing mankind off of the course?

Day 21:

Proverbs 20:5

The purposes of a person's heart are deep waters,

But one who has insight draws them out.

(Proverbs 20:5)

The heart, not the organ in your body, but your heart metaphorically speaking, is a very deep ocean of thoughts and feelings. It has purposes that many people do not understand or see.

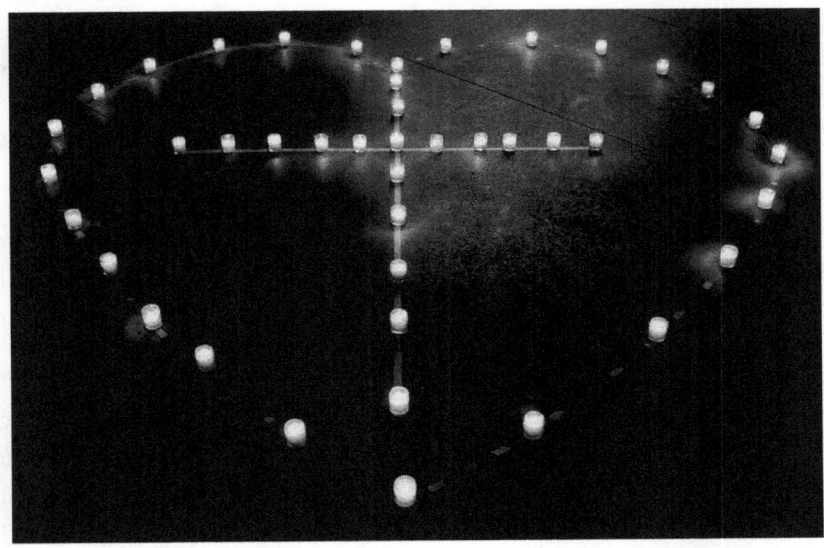

Within the heart, we have the ability to:

- Love
- Hate
- Care
- Feel loss
- Feel Fullness
- Feel happiness

While we understand these things, many of us don't understand the purposes of the heart.

Why do we fall in love with who we do? Ask anyone who has been through a bad relationship and they will tell you they don't understand it either. Sometimes, it seems like the heart leads us into the wrong direction. It is confusing and very hard to understand.

Wisdom

Have you ever met someone, though, who just seemed to have more insight into the heart? You probably have because we all know wise people. Wisdom and a person who is willing to listen to their wisdom will allow them to see into the purposes of the heart.

When you find yourself confused by a decision your heart led you to, there is nothing wrong with seeking out advice from the wise. That's because they will be able to give you insight that may have been just too confusing to you.

Yes, the actual purposes of the heart are like the depths of the ocean. They are unexplored, hard to see, and nearly invisible to the naked eye. However, humankind has found ways to explore those depths in the ocean. In the same manner, wise people have found ways to understand the purposes of the heart.

Final Thoughts

Think about your own heart and how well you understand its purposes:

> Did your heart lead you to do something that you don't understand?
>
> Have you considered that you learned something from what seemed like a wrong decision?
>
> What did you learn from that decision? Do you now see how the heart does have good purposes?

Day 22:

Mark 6:48-52

He saw the disciples straining at the oars, because the wind was against them. Shortly before dawn he went out to them, walking on the lake. He was about to pass by them, but when they saw him walking on the lake, they thought he was a ghost. They cried out, because they all saw him and were terrified.

Immediately, he spoke to them and said, 'Take courage! It is I. Don't be afraid.' Then he climbed into the boat with them, and the wind died down. They were completely amazed, for they had not understood about the loaves; and their hearts were hardened.

(Mark 6:48-52)

Because there are a couple of important things to discuss here, we will use this same scripture for the next two days.

In the first part, let's talk about walking on water and what that means in your life. Obviously, physics say that we cannot walk on water. The particles that make up water are loose and liquid. They cannot support our mass. If you try to walk on water, then you will simply sink.

However, there is another meaning to walking on water as well. It has to do with faith in yourself and faith in the race of humanity. As humans, we are capable of great things – things that cannot even be explained by physics or other forms of science.

Human Capability

For example, how is it that a mother can lift a car off her child? It makes no sense in the scientific world that a woman that barely weighs 120 pounds could perform such a feat. However, it has happened. That's because human beings are more powerful and more capable than we often give credit for.

You must have faith in yourself and your abilities. If you doubt yourself, then you will start to sink and this could negatively affect your efforts.

If you want to truly walk on water, then you have to believe in yourself. (Again, this is metaphorical. Please don't go out to a lake and attempt to actually walk on water). Believe in what you are capable of and you can accomplish more than you ever imagined.

Working Together

Can you imagine if all of humanity used their abilities and powers together? Think of all the things we could accomplish. Walking on water is just the beginning.

When we work together, each of us has a separate talent, ability, or power and working together means all of those different things come together to do great things in the world.

Final Thoughts

Walking on water isn't something that you could actually do, but there are many things that you can do and you may not realize it.

> Do you have a daunting task in front of you that you are afraid you will not be able to accomplish?
>
> What could you do to ensure you are able to believe in yourself so that you may "walk on water"?
>
> Do you think that humankind would be more capable of good things if we all came together and used our talents and gifts?

Day 23:

Mark 6: 48-52

He saw the disciples straining at the oars, because the wind was against them. Shortly before dawn he went out to them, walking on the lake. He was about to pass by them, but when they saw him walking on the lake, they thought he was a ghost. They cried out, because they all saw him and were terrified.

Immediately, he spoke to them and said, 'Take courage! It is I. Don't be afraid.' Then he climbed into the boat with them, and the wind died down. They were completely amazed, for they had not understood about the loaves; and their hearts were hardened.

(Mark 6:48-52)

Now, let's talk about calming the storm within yourself. It seems there are so many different things that can cause a storm. Just think about your life right now and consider what factors may be creating a storm within you (a struggle).

- A relationship problem

- Struggles with family, like parents or siblings
- Trouble at work with a coworker, a boss, or a customer
- Trouble letting go of past problems
- Difficulty in believing in yourself

The list could go on and on. Just think of the storms you may be facing. How have you been handling them? Storms can be difficult because you may not know what to do to rectify the situation. Remember that you do have the ability to calm the storm. All it takes is understanding that you have more powers and capabilities than you realize and then using those capabilities to handle the situation, whether it is a situation with someone else or a problem you are battling within yourself.

The Storms in the World

It always seems that the world is stormy, and this isn't referring to actual thunderstorms or hurricanes. Instead, it refers to worldly problems. If you look throughout history, you will see that there have been storms throughout the past.

- Wars date all the way back to ancient times.

- Hunger, poverty, and starvation have always been a problem for the human race.
- Crime dates back to the oldest manuscripts of written history. If you study the Bible, the first crime happened with Adam and Eve's children at the very beginning of mankind.
- Natural disasters have been around since the time of the dinosaurs.

Being a part of the human race means working toward calming those storms. Sometimes our efforts work better than others, but it is a fight we cannot give up. In your own race of life, you do have to consider what is happening in the world around you. You cannot simply focus on yourself. Instead, consider how you can contribute to attempts to calm the storms all over the world.

Final Thoughts

The storms can be calmed, no matter how big or small they may be. You simply need to understand your own power so that you can take charge and make the right decisions.

> Are you dealing with any storms right now in your life?
>
> What could you do differently to calm them?
>
> Are you contributing to calming the storms of humanity?

Day 24:

Genesis 1:26

Then God said, 'let us make mankind in our image, in our likeness,

So that they may rule over the fish in the sea and the birds in the sky,

Over the livestock and all the wild animals,

And all the creatures that move along the ground.' (Genesis 1:26)

In the race of life, we run on many different surfaces, including the sea. There are times when the race seems too hard or the troubles seem to be more than you can bear. During that time, you must remind yourself that as a human, you rule over all of the sea and land.

What It Means to Be a Ruler

Now that means something different than what you may realize. Consider a king who rules over a country. His job is to make decisions for the best of that country. His job is also to protect all of the people who live on the land. In other words, ruling something means more than just having power over it. It also means caring for it.

Since you rule over the sea, then you cannot let problems stand in your way. When you are weary from the race and the waters are choppy, when waves swell and lightning strikes, you still have power over the sea.

You can defeat those waves. You can walk on water. You can beat this leg of the race.

Caring for the Sea

At the same time that you take charge and control the stormy seas, you must take care of them as well. It is our job as humans to look after all parts of the earth. That is the only way we can be good caretakers and rulers.

Taking care of the sea means ensuring:

- It is safe from pollution
- It is not filled with garbage
- Endangered sea creatures are protected

The sea provides us important life. Through the sea, we are able to get nutrition in fish and other sea creatures. Additionally, the storms that provide rain and drinking water come from the seas. As good rulers, we must care for them properly.

Final Thoughts

This is the last day we will discuss this leg of the race. You have learned so much about racing on the waters, so consider these following final thoughts:

> Do you know how to overcome storms in your life? You have the ability. All you need to do is recognize it.

> Have you found yourself weary of the journey on the sea? Remember that you have power over it. You are a ruler of the sea, so take charge.

There are numerous troubles throughout the world for mankind. Part of your job is to use your abilities to help fight those troubles. What can you do to make a difference?

Part IV: The Air

Day 25:

Racing in the Air

The final leg of our race is in the air. Often, when people have physical air races, they are in airplanes, using gliders, or even in hot air balloons. We need some sort of machine or contraption to get us up in the air because we cannot fly on our own.

However, part of the human race of life does occur in the air. That's because the air, just like the land and the sea, is designed specifically to provide for us. The air gives us oxygen so that we may breathe and live. The air supports birds and other wildlife. It also allows the sunlight to travel to us so that plants and animals alike will be able to flourish.

The air is just as important as the land and the sea. It is also a good place to learn quite a few things about yourself and all of humankind.

Are you ready to begin your race in the air? Let's get started…

Day 26:

Proverbs 30:18-19

There are three things that are too amazing for me,

Four that I do not understand:

The way of an eagle in the sky,

The way of the snake on a rock,

The way of a ship on the high seas,

And the way of a man with a young woman.

(Proverbs 30:18-19)

There are many great mysteries in life, and we probably will never understand them fully. They will remain mysterious, wonderful, and

amazing to us. While you cannot fully comprehend how an eagle flies or how a snake moves even on hard surfaces, you can learn something from their wondrous capabilities.

Just think of the eagle. How does he fly? Animal specialists do understand the concept of it, but despite this, humanity has never learned how to create wings and get in the air without some sort of machine. It is somewhat of a mystery. However, that isn't all.

The Eagle

The eagle is such a magnificent creature that it has even become a symbol for the United States and for freedom. This bird, especially, understands the power of the air. Did you know that the eagle flies the best in storms? That's because the bird needs opposite wind currents to gain height and speed. The eagle will fly its greatest and most powerful flights even in the face of storms.

Think about this in your own life. You will face storms, but this could be your chance to fly your highest. When you remember that you are bigger than any problem that may come your way, you will find it much easier to use the storm to your advantage. After all, you can learn something from any problem you encounter in life.

Mankind

On January 12, 2010, an earthquake occurred in Haiti. It was an enormous quake and it killed 46,000 people. It injured hundreds of thousands more. People were left without homes, running water, and food. As soon as this happened, people from countries all over the world sprang into action. Food was sent. Doctors lent their skills. Even now, people travel to Haiti regularly to help rebuild all that was damaged or destroyed.

In the worst events of mankind, these are also the moments when humanity shows how strong it can actually be as a species. Just like the eagle that flies the strongest on storms, our species is the strongest in the face of tragedy.

Final Thoughts

The air is very powerful. It offers strength, life, and sustenance. The air can also be a force that drives us. When you observe the eagle and its strength in the storm, you must also think about your own strengths in the storm.

> What storm are you facing right now? Are you gaining strength from it or are you letting it blow you away?
>
> Think of all the times that humanity has come together in the face of storms and struggles. Can you think of more times when mankind showed its greatest strengths?

Day 27:

Isaiah 40:31

But those who hope in the Lord
Will renew their strength.
They will soar on wings like eagles;
They will run and not grow weary,
They will walk and not be faint. (Isaiah 40:31)

How often do you just want to go out and do something about an issue in your life? Patience can be a very hard virtue to maintain when you want to do something – take action. However, sometimes, it is not action that you need to take. There are times when you need to wait.

The Strengths of the Eagle

The eagle and other birds know how to use the air to their advantage. They fly when they need to, but they don't constantly stay in the air. They know when to rest, when to wait on the right wind current, and when to pick up their wings and soar.

You can learn something from this. Sometimes, when you try to force actions to take place, you actually harm yourself. You will become weary in the race of life and you may not feel like continuing to run it. Sometimes, you need to just wait and regain your strength.

In those times, when you do wait, you will find it much easier to regain the strength required to soar on the winds.

There are times when you do need to renew your strength. This is the best way to become strong enough to face anything that may come your way.

Final Thoughts

Think about your life and how much time you spend waiting or trying to force action to take place.

> Do you wait like you need to so that you may regain strength?
>
> What happens when you try to force action instead of waiting?
>
> What happens when you do wait and regain your strength? Do you find it easier to face the race of life?

Day 28:

Revelation 9:2

When he opened the Abyss, smoke rose from it like the smoke from a gigantic furnace.

The sun and sky were darkened by the smoke from the abyss.

(Revelation 9:2)

It would be nice if everyone and everything in the world was good, but that isn't the case. Unfortunately, there is darkness in the world. It tends to overshadow the good things from time to time and it certainly can cloud your vision.

Darkness is kind of like smoke. It rises up on the air. It is carried by the winds. Smoke can be seen through, but it blurs everything on the other side. Darkness has a way of doing the same thing.

Often, the bad things in the world can cloud your own life, make it hard to see the way through and make it difficult for you to remember that there are good things that you are racing for.

The Sunlight and Smoke

Have you ever noticed what the sunlight looks like when it filters through smoke? It is sometimes a little weaker than normal. It may look cloudy, but it is always there. It is always shining even when the smoke is in the way. In your life, the darkness may cloud your vision from time to time, but the good things are still there, filtering through. You just have to look and see them.

Darkness in the World

On earlier days, we went over some of the forms of darkness in the world, so there is no need to go over them in detail again. However, now, think of the darkness in the world like a cloud of smoke over people. Now, think about how we all still see the sunlight when we look for it. That's why good things always come out of the bad. People come together and work toward helping others in the face of disasters. Groups form to fight against crime. While there may be darkness, the sunlight and the good are always filtering through.

Final Thoughts

When you think of the bad things in your life and in the world as a cloud of smoke rising into the air, you will also learn how to deal with those things.

> Think of one source of darkness right now. Can you find ways to see the sunlight filtering through even though the smoke is thick?
>
> Now, focus on that sunlight. How can you use it to get through the problem and enjoy good things?

Day 29:

I Corinthians 9:26

Therefore I do not run like someone running aimlessly; I do not fight like a boxer bating the air.
(I Corinthians 9:26)

Running your race means doing more than just running around with no idea where you are going. When you don't have a goal or a plan, then you are doing no more good than a boxer who hits the air instead of his challenger.

When a boxer hits the air, they are hindering themselves in many ways. First, they are not accomplishing their goal (which is to box at the challenger). Additionally, they are using up their energy and getting tired for no reason whatsoever. You just can't do this in your own life and your own race.

Setting a Goal

Start thinking about your own life. If you have been boxing at the air, you should take the time and consider your goals. It doesn't matter what sort of goal you set, you need a reason to be running that race. Otherwise, you are just running aimlessly in circles.

By choosing a reason why you are running the race of life, you will be able to follow road signs and clear markers that will lead you toward your goal. If you don't have a reason, then you won't know what to look for and you could even end up going backwards, losing ground and essentially, boxing at the air. You will become weary and you will definitely become frustrated.

Others Boxing at the Air

Remember that part of running this race is helping others. Humanity is like a brotherhood. We often have opportunities to help others in their own races. It is our choice, though, whether we help or not. We can choose to keep running for ourselves, never looking to the side and never realizing that there are people floundering all around us. However, what kind of race is it if you allow others to get lost along the way?

Instead, we must choose to help those when we can. When you see someone boxing at the air or running aimlessly in circles, try to help them if you can. This could be as simple as paying for a meal for a homeless person, volunteering for a charity, or giving much-needed advice to someone confused.

Final Thoughts

Running a race means having goals and something to work toward. Otherwise, the race is simply running and boxing at the air.

>Do you have goals in your life?

>Are you working toward those goals or are you just boxing at the air?

>If you don't have goals, now is a good time to sit down and start thinking. These goals can be in work, relationships, family life, charity, or anything else. What goals will you set?

>Have you had an opportunity to help someone else boxing at the air?

>Have you taken the opportunity to help someone else or have you walked by? If you didn't help, how did that leave you feeling?

>What is one way you plan on taking action to help someone else in their race of life?

Day 30:

Matthew 6:26

Look at the birds in the air; they do not sow or reap or store away in barns,

Yet our heavenly Father feeds them.

Are you not much more valuable than they?

(Matthew 6:26)

There will be times in your life when you simply may not feel "good enough." It happens to us all. It could be at a time when you made a mistake at work or when you were invested in a relationship but they broke up with you. It could be when a loved one becomes ill or passes away and you feel like you could have or should have done something to stop this from happening.

In your race of life, bad things happen. This is a part of being human. You will face challenges and there will be times when you don't feel valuable. It is a human emotion and some people struggle with it more than others.

During those times, you may find yourself slowing down on that race. You may be tempted to just sit down and not even attempt to go further. This is especially true if you are questioning whether or not you are capable of accomplishing anything. However, there are some things you must remember.

The Birds in the Air

Look outside your window right now. Do you see any birds flying around? If that window is open, do you hear them singing? There is something very important you can learn from the birds in the air.

- They don't farm crops.
- They don't plant their own food.
- They don't make the scraps and branches they use for nests.
- They don't make money.

Somehow, though, they are provided with everything they need. The earth provides for them through wild growing seeds and grains and through branches or other materials they may use to make their nests.

Now ask yourself, are you not more valuable on this planet than the little birds flying through the air? Humanity has been given so many gifts and abilities that it is clear we hold great value on earth. We even have dominion over the animals and the plants. With that in mind, you must remind yourself that you are of such high value that you have been given gifts that no other living thing on this planet has.

You Will Be Taken Care Of

If the birds in the air are taken care of by the earth, then you will be too. Sometimes, that may be hard to see. However, when you are struggling, just remind yourself to look out the window. You are valuable in this world. You have a purpose. You have the ability to help yourself and to help others in their own race of life.

No matter how invaluable you may feel at one time or another, remember that this is just a feeling. It is not reality. Instead, the reality is that you will always be valuable.

Final Thoughts

Our own value as humans sometimes gets called into question, especially when something negative happens in our lives.

> Do you recognize your own value?
>
> Do you sometimes struggle with feeling like you are worthless?
>
> Can you name a few things that actually do show your value? (Accomplishments, loved ones, times when you have helped someone out, or anything else)
>
> Can you think of ways you could help others out when they are struggling with their own value?

Day 31:

Proverbs 27:8

A man who strays from home is like a bird that wanders from its nest.

(Proverbs 27:8)

We live in a society of wanting more. Every commercial you see on television. Every billboard you drive by on your way to work. Every person you speak to. They will all tell you the same thing: You must want more. You are expected to want a bigger house, a better job, more things, a better-looking mate, a fancier car. When you don't have those things, you are supposed to be unhappy and unsettled. This is what society has taught us.

However, this is not the truth of the race of life.

Life has been reduced to a lack of satisfaction. We are spending our time wanting, lusting after, and thinking that we need what others have. However, what does this accomplish for us? What, in the true race of life, do you gain from having a million-dollar home or a car that costs a hundred thousand dollars? When you have those things, you will find that you are still not satisfied. You will still want more.

That's the problem with this type of culture, and it is a problem that will most definitely pull you away from the race.

The Lesson of the Little Bird

When a bird is too young to fly, it is supposed to stay in the nest. But, there are times when those birds will be tempted to go out in the world on their own. They may see other birds flying. They may see a tasty-looking acorn on the tree branch. For whatever reason, they want more than what is offered in the safety of their nest, so they stray from it. Oftentimes, the result of this is devastating. The little bird will wander aimlessly away and will no longer have the safety of the nest and its parents to protect it.

When you lose track of your own goals and your own race in life, you could become like that little bird. Only for you, the things making you stray from your home could be money, objects, or the temptation of something bigger and better. It will only leave you wandering aimlessly.

It doesn't matter how much you "get," you will always want more. You will never find satisfaction in the simplicity of life itself.

Don't let yourself get derailed from the real importance in the race of life.

Final Thoughts

You do need to really evaluate your life. Determine if you are happy with having your necessities met or if you constantly want more.

> Do you find yourself lusting after things other people have?
>
> Do you want more even though you have enough right now?
>
> Can you think of a way to avoid straying from the nest so that you will continue on the proper path in your race?
>
> What can you do to remind yourself every day to be happy with what you have instead of dealing with the unhappiness of wanting what someone else has?

Day 32:

Psalm 55:6

I said, 'Oh, that I had the wings of a dove! I would fly away and be at rest.' (Psalm 55:6)

Often, people think of the dove as being a soft, sweet, innocent, and calm bird. People often associate the dove with peace, too. In the race of life, there may be times when you just wish you could have wings to carry you through the air away from your problems. After all, escaping seems to be a good option. However, this rarely works because we don't have wings like a dove. This is not the path to peace.

The Difference in the Dove

There is something you need to think about when considering the dove and its ability to fly away and get rest. When a dove flies and it becomes tired, it can use the strength of its other wing while he lets one rest. He doesn't have to alight upon a branch and possibly become prey to things that want to hurt him.

As humans, we don't have the same abilities as a bird in the air, but we can learn from it. We can learn the importance of knowing how to rest while still running our race. We can learn that sometimes, rest doesn't come from lying down or stopping, but from continuing on.

There is a difference in the dove when compared to other birds, especially birds of prey. It works through peace and quiet. It doesn't injure anyone, and doves actually have a good relationship with people.

You have to learn from the dove and be different from the people around you. You have to run a clean race, that is, and not do things to destroy or injure others just in an attempt to push yourself further.

Final Thoughts

There is a big difference between running away from problems and recognizing when you need to rest.

> Do you often wish that you could just fly away on the wings of a dove? What ways could you approach a situation that would allow you rest and would accomplish what you need to do?
>
> Do you understand the difference between resting when you need to and just sitting down and giving up on something?

Day 33:

Ezekiel 31:3b-6

Its top was among the clouds.

He waters made it grow, the deep made it high.

With its rivers it continually extended all around its planting place,

And it sent out its channels to all the trees in the field.

Therefore its height was loftier than all the trees in the field

And its boughs became many and its branches long

Because of the many waters as it spread them out

All the birds in the heavens nested in its boughs,

And under its branches all the beasts in the field gave birth,

And all the great nations lived under its shade.

(Ezekial 31:3b-6)

We have discussed the three parts of the race separately. We have talked about racing on land, in the air, and on the sea as if they are three totally separate things. There are different parts of the race of life and different things you will encounter. However, at the same time, they are all intertwined. Every leg of the race is for the same goal. Every decision you make will affect your present as well as your future.

The Tree

Just think of a tree. Think of an enormous oak tree that has been living and growing for hundreds of years. That tree depends on all three things to provide it life. Its limbs reach up to the sky, and the sunlight helps aid its growth and the creation of acorns. Its roots are securely founded in the land. Without that land, the tree would topple over. The sea provides water for rain and for moisture deep in the ground. Without that water, the tree would wither up and die.

You don't usually associate a tree with the sea because they must have land as an anchor; however, the sea is just as important a factor in the tree's growth.

Your Life

The same concept can be applied to your life. Every decision you make and every path you choose will actually be rooted in all three things: the land, the sea, and the air. You must draw from all parts of the race of humanity, not just one. After all, if you depend on one completely, you will be missing out on other things equally important in your life.

The old saying, "Don't miss the forest for the trees," definitely holds true in this case. When you focus on one thing, one problem, one goal, one person for too long, you will miss out on the whole scope of everything else: the ultimate purpose of your life.

Instead of doing this, you must be like the giant oak tree that knows how to depend on the water for sustenance, the sky for growth, and the land for an anchor. The tree uses all of these things equally. You can depend on all of the different factors in your life equally as well. When you do this, you will be able to see more, accomplish more, and help others in their own race more.

Final Thoughts

The race of life is much more than just the water or the land or the air. It involves all things equally.

> Do you spend too much time focusing on one thing in your life?
>
> Is this causing you to miss out on other things?
>
> Do you see the problems of people around you and help them when you can or are you too focused on one leg of the race to notice?

Day 34:

James 4:14

Why, you do not even know what will happen tomorrow. What is your life?

You are a mist that appears for a little while and then vanishes. (James 4:14)

Read it the wrong way and this scripture seems a little depressing. After all, our lives are likened to a breath of air. You know how quickly mist will rise up in the air, disperse, and then vanish. Thinking of your own life as that brief certainly isn't a happy consideration.

However, that isn't the purpose of this lesson. Instead, it is to help you gain a new perspective in how you think and what you do with your life. In your race, you will have numerous chances to stop and help others. There will be times when you could do something that may put you out but that may be extensively helpful to someone else.

If you focus too much on the importance of your own life, you may be tempted to ignore the fact that others need you and focus completely on yourself. However, that is certainly no legacy to leave behind once you are gone.

The Value of Life

You already know you are valuable. This is something you are taught by many different sources, and it is true. However, if you spend too much time *overvaluing* your life, you will come to think that you are more important than someone else. This is the root of arrogance.

When you consider that in the great scheme of things, your life is no more than a mist that dissipates into the air, you may begin to think differently.

- You are valuable, but so too is everyone else on this earth.

- You do not have unlimited time to make the right choices, do good things, and help others.

- You have to recognize the value that others offer as well as your own.

When you consider these things, you will find it significantly easier to do the right thing and help others instead of focusing solely on yourself and your own race.

Final Thoughts

When you consider your life and the value you place on it, you do have to ask yourself some difficult questions.

> Am I overvaluing myself and forgetting that others are valuable as well?

> Do I consider that others need my help sometimes, even when it may put me out?

> Do I understand that I am valuable, but so too is everyone else on the earth?

> Do I understand that I only have a certain amount of time on this earth to make a difference for others?

Day 35:

Job 12: 7-10

Ask the animals, and they will teach you, or the birds in the sky, and they will tell you;

Or speak to the earth, and it will teach you, or let the fish in the sea inform you.

Which of these does not know that the hand of the Lord has done this?

In his hand is the life of every creature and the breath of mankind.

(Job 12:7-10)

It's very easy to take things for granted when you have them available to you every day, but what if they were no longer there? What if they just stopped existing? This happens more than you may realize.

There is something that you can learn about your race in life from everything around you, including the birds in the air, the fish in the sea, and all creatures as well as plants and vegetation on earth. However, you may be ignoring those lessons.

You may not realize that the same things that create and form other life on the planet also form you. We are all connected and we must respect other living things. If we don't, we will miss out on so many important lessons.

However, even knowing this, you may not realize just how much you have been taking for granted:

"Scientists have estimated that over the course of Earth's history, anywhere between 1 and 4 billion species have existed on this planet. Be it through disease, genetic obsolescence, over-predation, or any number of factors, the overwhelming majority of these species are now extinct. Of these billions of species, roughly 50 million still survive in the modern era."   (Channel)

Just imagine the things you could have learned from the animals that no longer walk the earth. Take the time to learn from the creatures that still exist.

Look at the unfaltering love your pet dog offers and realize it would be a wonderful thing if we all had that kind of love for each other. Consider the lowly ant that works so hard for the good of the whole hill. There is so much to learn that you just cannot take creatures for granted.

Final Thoughts

Think about whether or not you have been taking anything for granted around you.

> Do you ever just stop and watch the birds in the trees?
>
> Have you learned anything from other living creatures in your life?
>
> Do you feel like you are taking things for granted when you could actually learn something from them?

Day 36:

Psalm 103:11

For as high as the heavens are above the earth,
So great is his love for those who fear him.
(Psalm 103:11)

How high is the sky? Where do you decide it stops? You could say that the sky or the "heavens" stop at the ozone layer or you could say it stops in our galaxy. However, technically, it appears to go on forever. Scientists have yet to find an end to the vast galaxies, star systems, and heavens that are all around us.

That's because they do not end. That's a hard thing for us to imagine because we don't know how to fathom something that actually goes to infinity. We can only understand something that has a beginning and an end because our lives have beginnings and ends.

Love Beyond End

As humans, we aren't truly capable of never-ending love. That's because too many flaws stand in our way. We can't just love someone for the fact that they are another human. However, this is certainly what we should strive toward.

You cannot put boundaries on the love you have for others. After all, they are struggling through the race of life just as you are. They need love, help, a chance in their own race.

Though you cannot actually love someone with no beginning and no end, you can make changes to the way you think about life.

Final Thoughts

Think to yourself about love. Think about it like the air and the sky that rises unendingly above Earth.

> Do you love other humans for the simple fact that they are struggling along a race as well?
>
> Do you think you could make changes in your life so that you show more love towards others?
>
> Do you think that the race of all humanity would be different if we showed more love toward each other?

Part V: The Race

Day 37:

Finishing the Race

You have learned about running all three parts of the race of life. You know how you could alter your choices, emotions, and thought processes to make better decisions. You have also learned just how important it is to help others along in their own race. After all, mankind could be thought of as a great brotherhood. We need each other. We also need the air, water, and land. We need the creatures on this earth. We even need the plants that grow out of the ground.

Without all of these things, we would have no race to run.

Hopefully you have the tools you need to run a better race in life. Now, let's finish up the last of our 40 day devotional with a few more important thoughts about running and finishing the race overall.

Day 38:

2 Timothy 4:7

I have fought the good fight, I have finished the race, I have kept the faith.

(2 Timothy 4:7)

There is much more to running the race than just trying to get somewhere. If you don't recognize that you need a reason to run and a goal in your race, then you will simply be running in circles.

If you have no path to follow, then you will have no reason to keep running the race in a way that would make you proud. You must consider how you will finish the race. Will you finish in a way that makes you proud and that leaves a good legacy on this earth or will you just limp along to the finish line with no real goal or legacy to leave for others?

Setting Goals

Take the time to actually sit down and set goals. What do you want to accomplish in life? This is a question you do need to answer. After all, when you do, you will run a race that you will be proud of. Ask yourself a few questions:

- Will I leave a good legacy from my race?
- Will I leave a reputation for making a positive difference on the earth?
- Do I want to finish the race in a way that will make me proud?

Once you answer those questions, you will be able to determine what changes you need to make in your life. This will lead you to complete a race of which you can be proud.

Final Thoughts

The race you are running in life has many different paths. You will spend your whole life choosing the right paths, making the right decisions, and finishing with pride. You need to ensure you make decisions throughout the race to finish the right way.

Sometimes, you will find it hard to keep the faith in the path you have chosen. Troubles and problems will come along and make you doubt yourself. However, as long as you remember that there is a much bigger reason why you are running the race, you will be able to keep that faith and finish with pride.

Day 39:

Acts 20:24

However, I consider my life nothing to me; my only aim is to finish the race and complete the task the Lord Jesus has given to me – the task of testifying to the good news of God's grace. (Acts 20:24)

Do you remember when we discussed the how vital it is to not put too much importance on your own life? This doesn't mean you

shouldn't recognize the value of who you are and what you are capable of.

In fact, you are very valuable. You are more important than other living creatures on the earth. You have rule over the planet, the seas, and the sky. Recognizing your value will help you see just how much you are capable of accomplishing for the good of others as well as yourself.

However, at the same time, you must recognize that every other human on this planet has the same value. They are just as capable, just as worthwhile, and just as special. Some of them don't have the advantages you do, but this is just another way you could choose to help others.

The Value of All Mankind

Recognizing the value of all mankind will help you understand what the race of life is truly about. It isn't an opportunity for you to "get ahead" or "get more." Instead, this race is about helping others and doing something good for mankind as a whole.

Final Thoughts

You have to consider why you are running the race of life in the first place so that you can determine the best way to finish strong.

> Do you recognize how valuable everyone is, including all of those around you?
>
> Do you know why you are running your race?
>
> Do you recognize that you are just as valuable as others?

Day 40:

Philippians 3:12-14

Not that I have already obtained all this, or have already arrived at my goal, but I press on to take hold of that for which Christ Jesus took hold of me. Brothers and sisters, I do not consider myself yet to have taken hold of it. But one thing I do: forgetting what is behind and straining toward what is ahead, I press on toward the goal to win the prize for which God has called me heavenward in Christ Jesus. (Philippians 3:12-14)

How often do we forget to follow the road ahead because we are so focused on things from the past? When you think about your own life, consider how many times you stay up at night worrying about something from yesterday or how often you cannot focus on your task at hand for worrying over something that happened months ago. Ask yourself:

- Do I worry about mistakes I made before?

- Do I find myself accomplishing little because I am too busy thinking about the past?
- Do I think about times when I have been hurt by others?

If you are like most people, then you answered yes to at least one or maybe even all three of these questions.

The Problem of Focusing on the Past

When you focus on the past, what can you accomplish today? Are you able to focus thoroughly on the tasks that are in front of you? The answer is no. That's because you are allowing your thoughts to focus on something that has already happened. You are remaining distracted and this keeps you from running the race in front of you.

The truth is there is nothing you can do about the past. You cannot change it. It is what it is. You can only learn from it and then move forward.

Part V: Day 40

The only way you can focus on the race that lies ahead of you is to leave the past behind. Do your best to forget about it and live only for what you can accomplish today, tomorrow, and the years in the future.

Final Thoughts

Running the race of life depends on making the best decisions you can and then learning from any mistakes that come along. Don't think of any problems, ordeals, or mistakes as something to dwell on and feel bad about. Instead, think of them as lessons that can lead you to make the right decisions in the future.

This is how you must run the race of life, and it is the most important lesson you can learn.

Conclusion

When you think of life as only something to be lived, you find it impossible to focus on goals, accomplish things, and help out others. When you think of life as a vast race, you will most certainly change what you put the most import on.

Take the time to look at the world around you. Recognize that there are so many people around you. Realize that they need help in their own race and know that they are just as valuable as you are.

By knowing that you do have something so important to accomplish in your life's race, you will be racing for a reason.

Remember too that you have opportunities to learn important and valuable lessons from everything around you on every leg of your race.

Hopefully you have learned just how important your life is and how much you could truly accomplish.

Go out and run a race to make yourself proud.

Works Cited

11 Facts About Global Poverty. (n.d.). Retrieved November 18, 2013, from Do Something: http://www.dosomething.org/tipsandtools/11-facts-about-global-poverty

2 Timothy 1:7. (n.d.). Retrieved November 18, 2013, from http://www.biblegateway.com/passage/?search=2+Timothy+1%3A7&version=NIV

2 Timothy 2:5. (n.d.). Retrieved November 19, 2013, from http://www.biblegateway.com/passage/?search=2+Tim++2:5

2 Timothy 4:7. (n.d.). Retrieved November 22, 2013, from http://www.biblegateway.com/passage/?search=2%20timothy%204:7&version=NIV

Act 20:24. (n.d.). Retrieved November 22, 2013, from http://www.biblegateway.com/passage/?search=acts%2020:24&version=NIV

Channel, D. (n.d.). *How Many Species Have Actually Gone Extinct?* Retrieved November 22, 2013, from Curiosity: http://curiosity.discovery.com/question/how-species-actually-gone-extinct

Ecclesiastes 1:6-7. (n.d.). Retrieved November 20, 2013, from http://www.biblegateway.com/passage/?search=ecclesiastes%201:6-7&version=NIV

Ecclesiastes 9:11-12. (n.d.). Retrieved November 18, 2013, from http://www.raystedman.org/daily-devotions/ecclesiastes/who-wins-the-race

Ezekial 31:3b-6. (n.d.). Retrieved November 21, 2013, from http://www.biblegateway.com/passage/?search=Ezekial%2031:3-8&version=NASB

Galatians 5:7. (n.d.). Retrieved November 19, 2013

Genesis 1:26. (n.d.). Retrieved November 21, 2013, from http://www.biblegateway.com/passage/?search=Genesis+1%3A1%2CGenesis+1%3A26&version=NIV

Genesis 1:9-10. (n.d.). Retrieved November 19, 2013, from http://www.biblegateway.com/passage/?search=Gen%201:9-Gen%201:10

(n.d.). I Corinthians 9:24-27. In The Bible (New International Version).

I Corinthians 9:26. (n.d.). Retrieved November 21, 2013, from http://www.biblegateway.com/passage/?search=I%20corinthians%209:26&version=NIV

Isaiah 40:31. (n.d.). Retrieved November 21, 2013, from http://www.biblegateway.com/passage/?search=isaiah%2040:31&version=NIV

James 4:14. (n.d.). Retrieved November 22, 2013, from http://www.biblegateway.com/passage/?search=James+4%3A14

Jeremiah 5:22. (n.d.). Retrieved November 19, 2013, from https://www.biblegateway.com/passage/?search=Jer%205:22

Job 12:7-10. (n.d.). Retrieved November 22, 2013, from http://www.biblegateway.com/passage/?search=Job%2012:7-10&version=NIV

Job 26:10. (n.d.). Retrieved November 20, 2013, from http://www.biblegateway.com/passage/?search=job%2026:10&version=NIV

John 16:33. (n.d.). Retrieved November 18, 2013, from http://www.biblegateway.com/passage/?search=John+16%3A33

Mark 6:48-52. (n.d.). Retrieved November 21, 2013, from http://www.biblegateway.com/passage/?search=Mark%206:48-52&version=NIV

Matthew 6:26. (n.d.). Retrieved November 21, 2013, from http://www.biblegateway.com/passage/?search=Matthew+6%3A26

Micah 7:19. (n.d.). Retrieved November 20, 2013, from http://www.biblegateway.com/passage/?search=micah%207:19&version=NIV

Nations Compared. (n.d.). Retrieved November 18, 2013, from Nation Master: http://www.nationmaster.com/graph/cri_rap-crime-rapes

Organization, W. H. (2013). *World Health Statistics 2013*.

Philippians 3:12-14. (n.d.). Retrieved November 22, 2013, from http://www.biblegateway.com/passage/?search=philippians%203:12-14&version=NIV

Philippians 3:14. (n.d.). Retrieved November 19, 2013, from http://www.biblegateway.com/passage/?search=philippians+3:14

Proverbs 12:10. (n.d.). Retrieved November 20, 2013, from http://www.biblegateway.com/passage/?search=Porverbs%2012:10&version=NIV

Proverbs 20:5. (n.d.). Retrieved November 20, 2013, from http://www.biblegateway.com/passage/?search=Proverbs%2020:5&version=NIV

Proverbs 27:23-24. (n.d.). Retrieved November 19, 2013, from http://www.biblegateway.com/passage/?search=Porverbs%2027:23-24&version=NIV

Proverbs 27:8. (n.d.). Retrieved November 21, 2013, from http://www.biblegateway.com/passage/?search=Proverbs%2027:8&version=NIV

Proverbs 30:18-19. (n.d.). Retrieved November 21, 2013, from http://www.biblegateway.com/passage/?search=Proverbs%2030:18-20&version=NIV

Proverbs 6:6-8. (n.d.). Retrieved November 20, 2013, from http://www.biblegateway.com/passage/?search=Proverbs%206:6-8&version=NIV

Psalm 103:11. (n.d.). Retrieved November 22, 2013, from http://www.biblegateway.com/passage/?search=psalm%20103:11&version=NIV

Psalm 119:71. (n.d.). Retrieved November 18, 2013, from http://www.biblegateway.com/passage/?search=Psalm%20119:71

Psalm 55:6. (n.d.). Retrieved November 21, 2013, from http://www.biblegateway.com/passage/?search=Ps.55.6

Psalm 104:5. (n.d.). Retrieved November 20, 2013, from http://www.biblegateway.com/passage/?search=Psalm%20104:5&version=NIV

Revelation 9:2. (n.d.). Retrieved November 21, 2013, from http://www.biblegateway.com/passage/?search=revelation%209:2&version=NIV

Photographic Sources

In order of appearance:

http://commons.wikimedia.org/wiki/File:2011_Chicago_Marathon_runners.jpg

http://commons.wikimedia.org/wiki/File:KSUMACCG3.JPG

http://commons.wikimedia.org/wiki/File:Gila_trout_fish_in_net.jpg

http://commons.wikimedia.org/wiki/File:Jim_Thorpe_olympic.png

http://commons.wikimedia.org/wiki/File:Orphans_from_the_Home_and_Life_center_in_Phuket,_Thailand,_press_their_hands_into_cement_for_a_monument_that_is_being_built_as_part_of_a_community_service_project_with_the_crew_of_the_aircraft_carrier_USS_Nimitz_130530-N-WM477-328.jpg

http://commons.wikimedia.org/wiki/File:Do_Not_Cross,_Crime_Scene.jpg

http://commons.wikimedia.org/wiki/File:Boston_Marathon_explosions_(8652957509).jpg

http://commons.wikimedia.org/wiki/File:Mother_and_Child_(Imagicity_455).jpg

http://commons.wikimedia.org/wiki/File:Family_eating_at_a_table_(2).jpg

http://upload.wikimedia.org/wikipedia/commons/6/6c/Hurdles_%28Scenes_from_a_Track_Meet%29.jpg

http://commons.wikimedia.org/wiki/File:Barricade_blinkers.jpg

http://commons.wikimedia.org/wiki/File:Lance-Armstrong-TdF2004.jpg

http://upload.wikimedia.org/wikipedia/commons/thumb/0/09/Radar_speed_sign_-_close-up_-_under_limit.jpg/120px-Radar_speed_sign_-_close-up_-_under_limit.jpg

http://commons.wikimedia.org/wiki/File:Kid_playing_soccer.jpg

http://commons.wikimedia.org/wiki/File:Tennis_shake_hands_after_match.jpg

http://upload.wikimedia.org/wikipedia/commons/thumb/e/eb/Moe_Epsilon%27s_blue_ribbon.jpg/111px-Moe_Epsilon%27s_blue_ribbon.jpg

http://commons.wikimedia.org/wiki/File:US_Navy_070716-N-9195K-052_Kenny_Kwon,_a_volunteer_from_the_University_of_California_at_San_Diego%5Ersquo,s_Pre-Dental_Society,_assists_Dr._Hoang_Thu_Ha,_a_dentist_with_the_East_Meets_West_Foundation,_as_he_places_sealant_on_a_lo.jpg

http://upload.wikimedia.org/wikipedia/commons/thumb/c/c7/Vegetable_garden_detail.jpg/120px-Vegetable_garden_detail.jpg

http://commons.wikimedia.org/wiki/File:Whataroa_River_mouth.jpg

http://commons.wikimedia.org/wiki/File:WAVES.jpg

http://commons.wikimedia.org/wiki/File:2011-13_Acre_sea_wall.JPG

http://commons.wikimedia.org/wiki/File:Low_Tide_Darwin.jpg

http://commons.wikimedia.org/wiki/File:Stormy_Waters_-_geograph.org.uk_-_1250999.jpg

http://commons.wikimedia.org/wiki/File:Gift_House.jpg

http://upload.wikimedia.org/wikipedia/commons/thumb/3/3f/Trash_Recycling_with_Disposal_Containers.jpg/120px-Trash_Recycling_with_Disposal_Containers.jpg

http://commons.wikimedia.org/wiki/File:New_York_electricity_sources_2010.svg

http://commons.wikimedia.org/wiki/File:USDA_sheep.jpg

http://upload.wikimedia.org/wikipedia/commons/thumb/3/36/Animal_Welfare_Mobile_Clinic%2C_SPCA_%28Hong_Kong%29.JPG/120px-Animal_Welfare_Mobile_Clinic%2C_SPCA_%28Hong_Kong%29.JPG

http://upload.wikimedia.org/wikipedia/commons/thumb/5/50/Feeding_puppy_dogs.jpg/120px-Feeding_puppy_dogs.jpg

http://upload.wikimedia.org/wikipedia/commons/thumb/5/54/20131203_kitten_B.jpg/120px-20131203_kitten_B.jpg

http://upload.wikimedia.org/wikipedia/commons/thumb/f/f1/Lasius_Niger.jpg/120px-Lasius_Niger.jpg

http://upload.wikimedia.org/wikipedia/commons/thumb/b/b7/Leaf_cutter_ants_CostaRica.jpg/120px-Leaf_cutter_ants_CostaRica.jpg

http://upload.wikimedia.org/wikipedia/commons/thumb/3/39/He_Laid_the_Foundation_of_the_Earth.jpg/120px-He_Laid_the_Foundation_of_the_Earth.jpg

http://upload.wikimedia.org/wikipedia/commons/thumb/8/89/Cyclone_Catarina_from_the_ISS_on_March_26_2004.JPG/120px-Cyclone_Catarina_from_the_ISS_on_March_26_2004.JPG

http://commons.wikimedia.org/wiki/File:2010_Baumwurzel.JPG

http://commons.wikimedia.org/wiki/File:Yacht_race_off_Inverkip_-_geograph.org.uk_-_1424201.jpg

http://commons.wikimedia.org/wiki/File:Borda_do_mundo_(4942486361).jpg

http://commons.wikimedia.org/wiki/File:A_Winter_Storm_at_Strandhill_-_geograph.org.uk_-_1050818.jpg

http://commons.wikimedia.org/wiki/File:Paranal_and_the_Shadow_of_the_Earth.jpg

http://commons.wikimedia.org/wiki/File:Fifi_shipwreck.jpg

http://commons.wikimedia.org/wiki/File:Fish,_a_lot_of_fish_(2152054969).jpg

http://commons.wikimedia.org/wiki/File:Mossman_River_and_Gorge.JPG

http://upload.wikimedia.org/wikipedia/commons/thumb/b/b5/USACE_Tillamook_Bay_Oregon.jpg/120px-USACE_Tillamook_Bay_Oregon.jpg

http://commons.wikimedia.org/wiki/File:God_is_Love.JPG

http://commons.wikimedia.org/wiki/File:Hands_put_over_another.jpg

http://commons.wikimedia.org/wiki/File:Wall_cloud_with_lightning_-_NOAA.jpg

http://commons.wikimedia.org/wiki/File:Gulmarg_-_Srinagar_views_34.JPG

http://upload.wikimedia.org/wikipedia/commons/thumb/3/3c/Workers_clean_up_after_oil_spill_on_coast.jpg/120px-Workers_clean_up_after_oil_spill_on_coast.jpg

http://commons.wikimedia.org/wiki/File:NRCSFL97013(15588)(NRCS_Photo_Gallery).jpg

http://commons.wikimedia.org/wiki/File:Hotair_balloons_amk.jpg

http://commons.wikimedia.org/wiki/File:Haliaeetus_leucocephalus2.jpg

http://upload.wikimedia.org/wikipedia/commons/thumb/b/b4/Haliaeetus_leucocephalus-ad-flight-USFWS.jpg/120px-Haliaeetus_leucocephalus-ad-flight-USFWS.jpg

http://upload.wikimedia.org/wikipedia/commons/thumb/2/2f/Haiti_Earthquake_building_damage.jpg/120px-Haiti_Earthquake_building_damage.jpg

http://commons.wikimedia.org/wiki/File:Buteo_albicaudatus_-_Gravata,_Pernambuco,_Brazil.jpg

http://upload.wikimedia.org/wikipedia/commons/thumb/c/c6/Kanaga_Volcano%2C_Kanaga_Island%2C_Aleutians.jpg/120px-Kanaga_Volcano%2C_Kanaga_Island%2C_Aleutians.jpg

http://upload.wikimedia.org/wikipedia/commons/thumb/6/60/USMC-110912-M-SO228-182.jpg/80px-USMC-110912-M-SO228-182.jpg

http://commons.wikimedia.org/wiki/File:Flock_of_birds_over_piggery_-_geograph.org.uk_-_301441.jpg

http://upload.wikimedia.org/wikipedia/commons/thumb/c/c1/Baby_birds_in_nest.jpg/120px-Baby_birds_in_nest.jpg

http://upload.wikimedia.org/wikipedia/commons/thumb/8/85/Columbina_passerina.jpg/120px-Columbina_passerina.jpg

http://upload.wikimedia.org/wikipedia/commons/thumb/6/68/General_Sherman_Tree_2.JPG/80px-General_Sherman_Tree_2.JPG

http://upload.wikimedia.org/wikipedia/commons/thumb/4/45/Oberfallenberg_11.jpg/120px-Oberfallenberg_11.jpg

http://upload.wikimedia.org/wikipedia/commons/thumb/0/0e/School_of_fish_at_California_Academy_of_Sciences.JPG/120px-School_of_fish_at_California_Academy_of_Sciences.JPG

http://upload.wikimedia.org/wikipedia/commons/thumb/1/12/Photographers_in_a_flock_of_birds.jpg/120px-Photographers_in_a_flock_of_birds.jpg

http://upload.wikimedia.org/wikipedia/commons/thumb/4/49/Cyprus-6-21-2010.jpg/120px-Cyprus-6-21-2010.jpg

http://commons.wikimedia.org/wiki/File:Pittsburgh_Marathon_Finish_Line_2010.jpg

All photos are licensed under Creative Commons and free to share and remix as long as the new product is also made available to share alike.

www.ingramcontent.com/pod-product-compliance
Lightning Source LLC
Chambersburg PA
CBHW070640050426
42451CB00008B/241